13 Colonies

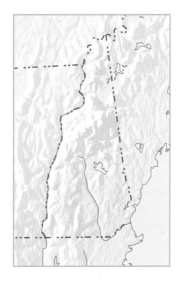

New Hampshire

13 Colonies

NEW HAMPSHIRE

THE HISTORY OF NEW HAMPSHIRE COLONY, 1623–1776

ROBERTA WIENER AND JAMES R. ARNOLD

Raintree

Chicago, Illinois

For information, address the publisher:

Raintree, 100 N. LaSalle, Suite 1200, Chicago, IL 60602

Printed in China by South China Printing.

09 08 07 06 05

10 9 8 7 6 5 4 3 2 1

Library of Congress Cataloging-in-Publication Data

Cataloging-in-publication data is on file with the Library of Congress.

Disclaimer

All the Internet addresses (URLs) given in this book were valid at the time of going to press. However, due to the dynamic nature of the Internet, some addresses may have changed, or sites may have changed or ceased to exist since publication. While the author and publishers regret any inconvenience this may cause readers, no responsibility for any such changes can be accepted by either the author or the publishers.

The paper used to print this book comes from sustainable resources.

Some words are shown in bold, **like this.** You can find out what they mean by looking in the glossary.

Title page: Portsmouth in the 1770s

Opposite: The rocky New England coast

The authors wish to thank Walter Kossmann, whose knowledge, patience, and ability to ask all the right questions have made this a better series.

PICTURE ACKNOWLEDGMENTS

COURTESY AMERICAN ANTIQUARIAN SOCIETY: 8, 34 ARCHITECT OF THE CAPITOL: 7 AUTHORS: 11, 49 right (courtesy of Guilford Courthouse National Military Park) ANNE S.K. BROWN MILITARY COLLECTION, BROWN UNIVERSITY LIBRARY, PROVIDENCE, RI: 44 top WILLIAM CULLEN BRYANT, et. al., *Scribner's Popular History of the United States*, 1896: Title page, 25, 27 bottom COLONIAL WILLIAMSBURG FOUNDATION: 9, 30, 51 U.S. GOVERNMENT PRINTING OFFICE: 57 *Harper's New Monthly Magazine*: 55 *Howard Pyle's Book of the American Spirit*, 1923: 32, 43 LIBRARY OF CONGRESS: 12, 21, 24, 28-29, 44-45, 47 top, 53 NATIONAL ARCHIVES: 39 bottom, 42, 48, 50, 56 NATIONAL PARK SERVICE, COLONIAL NATIONAL HISTORICAL PARK: Cover, 14-15, 19, 22, 37 top, 38-39 NEW HAMPSHIRE HISTORICAL SOCIETY: 16-17, 17 bottom, 18, 20, 23, 33, 36, 40, 41, 49 left, 52, 54, 59 I.N. PHELPS STOKES COLLECTION, NEW YORK PUBLIC LIBRARY: 10, 46-47 M. NIGRO: 5, 13 COURTESY OF THE NORTH CAROLINA OFFICE OF ARCHIVES AND HISTORY: 37 bottom PHILADELPHIA FREE LIBRARY: 31 U.S. SENATE COLLECTION: 6

CONTENTS

Prologue: The World in 1623

In 1623, the first employees of the Laconia Company built a small settlement on the coast of New Hampshire. Encouraged by the survival of Jamestown, Virginia, and reports by English explorers, the prosperous merchants of the Laconia Company believed they could further enrich themselves by investing in a colonial venture. The investors chose a cold and difficult place in which to pursue their dreams of wealth, but life in a cold North American climate had already been proven possible by the English in Newfoundland and the French in Nova Scotia and Quebec.

The first European explorers to set foot in North America had been the Vikings of northern Europe. They visited a site on the coast of modern-day Canada some time before the year 1000. The Vikings preceded other Europeans in America by almost 500 years, but they did not stay there for long. By the time Europeans again began to explore the wider world, the Viking explorations had faded from memory.

According to popular legend, the Norwegian Viking, Leif Erikson, was the first European ever to set foot in America. He was one of the first, but probably not the very first. An Icelandic explorer may have beaten him there by more than ten years. The Vikings are said to have given the name Vinland to a part of North America.

During the Renaissance, a 150-year period of invention and discovery beginning during the 1400s, advances in navigation and the building of better sailing ships allowed longer voyages. A new age of exploration began, with great seamen from Portugal, Spain, Italy, the Netherlands, France, and England sailing into uncharted waters. The explorers reached Africa, India, the Pacific Ocean, China, Japan, and Australia. They encountered kingdoms and civilizations that had existed for centuries.

The voyages from Europe to these distant shores went around Africa. This made the trip long and dangerous. So, European explorers began to sail westward in search of shortcuts. In 1492, the explorer Christopher Columbus landed on an island on the far side of the Atlantic Ocean and claimed it for Spain. He thought that he had actually sailed all the way around the world and come to an island near India. Years of exploration by numerous sailors passed before the people of Europe realized that Columbus had been the first European of their era to set foot in a land unknown to them. They called this forgotten

Many artists have imagined and made pictures of Columbus coming ashore on the far side of the Atlantic after making the crossing from Europe.

NEW WORLD: WESTERN
HEMISPHERE OF EARTH,
INCLUDING NORTH
AMERICA, CENTRAL
AMERICA, AND SOUTH
AMERICA; SO CALLED
BECAUSE THE PEOPLE OF THE
OLD WORLD, IN EUROPE,
DID NOT KNOW ABOUT THE
EXISTENCE OF THE AMERICAS
UNTIL THE 1400S

land the **New World**, although it was not new to the people who lived there. After Columbus, Amerigo Vespucci claimed to have reached the New World. Whether he actually did or not, in 1507 a mapmaker put his name on a map, and the New World became America, or the Americas. Still looking for a shortcut to the riches of Asia, European explorers continued to sail to North and South America. They began to claim large pieces of these lands for their own nations.

The first English ship to cross the Atlantic Ocean was commanded by the Italian-born John Cabot in 1497. Cabot's exploration of the eastern coast of Canada formed

the basis for all of England's future claims to American colonies. A succession of explorers made landfall on the eastern coast of North America, and several of them explored the New England coast. The Italian seaman, Giovanni da Verrazano, commanded a French expedition in 1524 and explored and charted the coast from the Carolinas to Maine.

After several voyages, in 1583 Sir Humphrey Gilbert claimed the fishing camps and fur trading posts on the coast of Newfoundland as an English colony. Soon after, he disappeared at sea, leaving his royal patent, or permission, to explore and trade in America to his half brother, Walter Raleigh. Raleigh began sponsoring expeditions to America and claimed for England a large area of land he called Virginia. The disappearance of his colonists from Roanoke Island some time after 1587 remains an enduring mystery.

In 1602, Englishman Bartholomew Gosnold made a successful voyage to the New England coast. Gosnold and his men decided they did not have enough food to stay and establish a colony, so they returned to England with a ship full of valuable furs, logs, and **sassafras** roots. Gosnold was followed in 1603 by the 23-year-old English sailor Martin Pring, also in search of sassafras and other trade goods. In 1605, Sir George Waymouth sailed along the coast from Nantucket to Maine. He brought back five Abenakis—**Native Americans** from Maine—and glowing reports of a rich and beautiful land, as indeed it was in summertime. In England, the Abenakis were dressed in English clothes and taught to speak English. They were given speeches to memorize that publicized the wonders of their native land.

The French explorer Samuel de Champlain then spent two years charting the New England coast and searching out a site for a French colony, but hard winters and French politics conspired to defeat his efforts. Members of the Virginia Company, which had founded the colony at Jamestown in 1607, at the same time sponsored a New

NATIVE AMERICAN: MEMBER OF NUMEROUS GROUPS OF PEOPLE WHO HAD BEEN LIVING IN AMERICA FOR THOUSANDS OF YEARS AT THE TIME THAT THE FIRST EUROPEANS ARRIVED

Opposite: English fishermen had been fishing the Grand Banks off Newfoundland since the late 1500s.

James I ruled England from 1603 until 1625.

England colony on the coast of Maine. This colony failed because, after one winter, the settlers found life too harsh. The unsuccessful colonists returned to England in 1608.

Former Virginia colonist Captain John Smith explored and mapped the coast of New England in 1614. Smith's account of his voyage raised interest in the region's great trees and plentiful fish, so King James I claimed the area for England. King James's son, the future King Charles I, named the area New England. In 1620, King James set up the Council of New England to supervise the settlement and government of a territory whose borders were to extend all the way to the Pacific Ocean.

Captain John Smith made an accurate map of the New England coast on his 1614 voyage. The Isles of Shoals off the New Hampshire coast, which he visited, were originally called Smith's Isles.

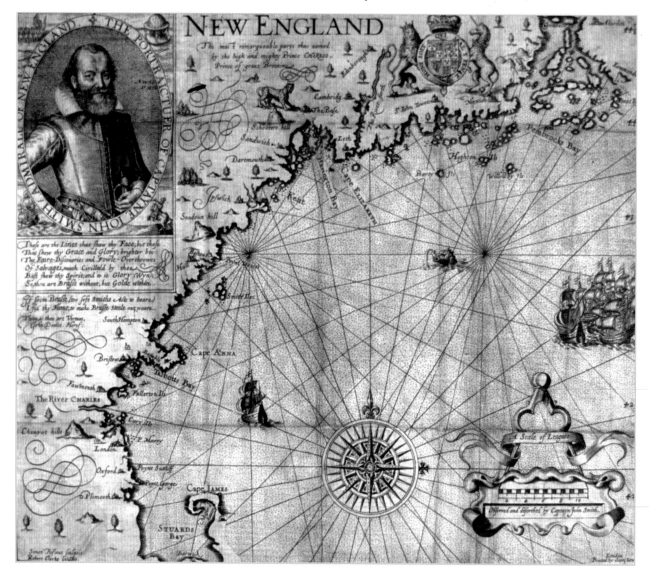

I.
IN SEARCH OF LAKES AND RICHES

The Council of New England consisted of 40 stockholders, with Sir Ferdinando Gorges as its president. Gorges had become interested in colonizing New England due to his family's friendship with the families of Humphrey Gilbert and Walter Raleigh. In addition, three of the Abenakis brought to England by Sir George Waymouth had been guests in Gorges' home.

Gorges joined with Captain John Mason to sponsor English settlements in New England. Mason had been governor of Newfoundland from 1615 to 1621. He proposed establishing a colony with settlements consisting of about 70 settlers each. Mason planned to supply them with food, tools, and livestock. In partnership with Gorges, in 1621 Mason received a grant of land on which to carry out his ideas. The grant's borders were poorly defined, since none of the grantees had ever set foot on the land. The following year, Mason and Gorges formed the Laconia Company with a group of English merchants.

The company's name, Laconia, referred to the "Lake of the Iroquois." The French explorer, Samuel de Champlain, had described this land but no Englishman had seen it. This lake country, possibly the area around the lake now known as Lake Champlain, was believed to be

The guns of Fort Ticonderoga, overlooking Lake Champlain. The French built Fort Ticonderoga in 1755. Whether or not Lake Champlain was the fabled "Lake of the Iroquois," the British and French in America saw the importance of its central location and fought for control of it. When the American colonists rebelled against Great Britain, they, too, fought for the lake.

the key to controlling everything of value in the entire region—the rivers, access to beaver furs, and trade with the Native Americans. The company's investors hoped the settlers would find this fabled lake country and deny French and Dutch traders access to it. They also hoped to gain great wealth from the furs and salted fish that the settlers would send them.

How did Gorges, Mason, and their investors find people willing to transplant themselves to this cold and rocky soil? For most people, life in England in the early 1600s was hard. Wealthy people had taken over much of the rural land, forcing poor people to leave the countryside and move to urban centers to search for jobs. During the early part of the century London grew by more than fifty percent. Crowded conditions hastened the spread of deadly diseases, including the terrible bubonic plague. Conditions were so bad that some people were willing to face the unknown in America rather than stay in England.

In 1623, the Laconia Company began sending groups of hardy settlers to the banks of New Hampshire's Piscataqua River, near where it drained into the ocean. They built several small settlements under the leadership of a military man, Walter Neale, and David Thomson and the brothers Edward and William Hilton, fish dealers from the southwestern coast of England. Each group of settlers arrived with seeds; equipment for fishing, lumbering, and salt production; and trade goods including blankets, metal tools and pots, and liquor. In the first two years of settlement, 66 men and 22 women arrived from England as employees of the Company.

New Hampshire's settlers needed a constant supply of salt to preserve meat and fish. Salt was made by boiling down salty water and then letting the salt settle to the bottom of the pot. The trees for miles around the salt works were cut down to fuel the constant fires. The colonists built salt works at the site of any salt spring they found, but still, they sometimes had to import salt.

2.
NEW HAMPSHIRE IN 1623

The first European explorers and settlers to see New Hampshire saw thick woods. Not one acre in 6,000 was open land. Anyone who hoped to build a house or grow and harvest crops first had to cut down trees—oak, sugar maple, beech, birch, pine, spruce, and cedar. The next great task facing them was to pull rocks from the ground. The woods were full of bear, moose, and deer, hunted for meat, and mink, fox, and beaver, desired for their fur. Large flocks of ducks, geese, and loons lived on the lakes and rivers.

The modern day state of New Hampshire borders on Maine, the Atlantic Ocean, Massachusetts, Vermont, and the Canadian province of Quebec. Much of the land was shaped by glaciers. The Connecticut River, which begins in a lake in northern New Hampshire, forms the border with Vermont, and New Hampshire's best farmland lies along its banks. The Merrimack River flows southward down the center of the state.

New Hampshire has eighteen miles of seacoast and a small corner of coastal lowland, which extends about twenty miles inland from the ocean. Offshore lie the Isles of

The rocky New England coast

13

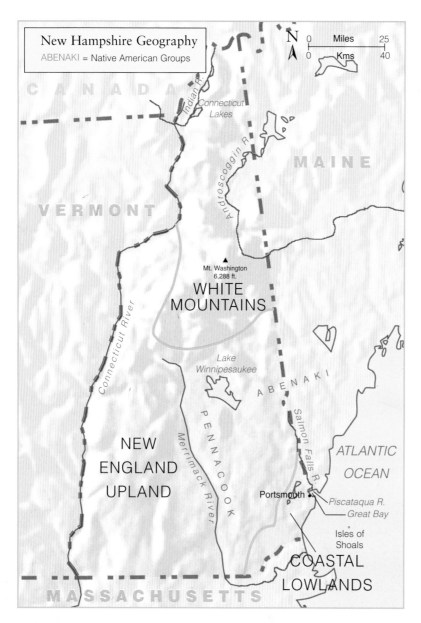

New Hampshire Geography
ABENAKI = Native American Groups

N

Miles 0 — 25
Kms 0 — 40

CANADA

Indian R.

Connecticut Lakes

Androscoggin R.

MAINE

VERMONT

Mt. Washington 6,288 ft.

WHITE MOUNTAINS

Connecticut River

Lake Winnipesaukee

ABENAKI

PENNACOOK

Salmon Falls R.

NEW ENGLAND UPLAND

Merrimack River

ATLANTIC OCEAN

Portsmouth

Piscataqua R.
Great Bay

Isles of Shoals

COASTAL LOWLANDS

MASSACHUSETTS

Shoals, which were to become a base for English fishing operations. Several streams and rivers flow into the saltwater Great Bay. From the Great Bay, the Piscataqua River flows into the ocean. At the northern end of the coast is the state's one deep-water harbor, around which the town of Portsmouth grew. Beyond the coastal lowland, the New England Upland rises, with its rolling hills, more than 1,000 lakes, and granite deposits. Farther north are the White Mountains, with several peaks more than a mile high. The highest is Mount Washington at 6,288 feet (1,916 meters).

The climate is slightly warmer near the coast and very cold farther inland. Winter temperatures are about 25°F (–4°C) near the coast and can drop well below zero in the mountains. The mountains receive as much as 100 inches (254 centimeters) of snow each winter. Melting snow provides much of the state's water, with only a moderate amount of rain in the summer. Summers are fairly cool, averaging about 70°F (21°C).

During the long winters, people cut large blocks of ice from frozen lakes, kept them in a cool place all winter, and used them to keep food cold as the weather warmed.

Native Americans first lived in the region about 10,000 years ago. The largest group living in the future colony of New Hampshire was the Algonquian-speaking Pennacook, led by the **sachem** Passaconaway. About 3,000 Pennacooks lived in southern and central New Hampshire by the year 1600. About another 1,000 Algonquian-speakers belonged to smaller bands, including the Abenaki of eastern New Hampshire and western Maine. A great epidemic swept through the Native Americans of the New England coast

Both the native people and the colonists tapped maple trees for the sweet syrup.

SACHEM: ALGONQUIAN WORD FOR CHIEF

around 1617. The cause and the disease are unknown, but it was possibly brought by the early European explorers. As many as a third of all the Native Americans on the northern New England coast died before the first English people settled among them.

The Pennacook lived like other Algonquian speakers throughout eastern North America, but adapted some of their ways to the cold climate of New England. They spent some of their time in villages of 50 to 200 people, living in wigwams built of bark-covered bent poles. They hung furs on the inside walls to help keep warm during the long winters. The women grew corn, beans, squash, and pumpkins, and gathered berries and nuts. Women were also responsible for making deerskin clothing. They used dyed porcupine quills to decorate the garments. They made cloaks of fur to wear in wintertime. Men hunted, made canoes, and fished with spears. In the winter they made holes in the ice to catch fish from lakes. The Pennacook also tapped sugar maple trees for sap, from which they made syrup and sugar.

The Algonquians needed to be able to travel in all seasons. New Hampshire's many streams and rivers served as highways through the forest. To move along these highways, the Algonquians built light but sturdy canoes out of birchbark stitched onto cedar wood frames. Their canoes could withstand the choppy water often found in large lakes and bays. The canoes were light enough to carry, or portage, around rapids and waterfalls. In the winter, the Algonquians walked across the snow's surface by using snow shoes. Sleds replaced canoes as a means of hauling heavy loads. They lived by planting crops in the spring, fishing and gathering in the summer, harvesting their crops in the fall, and hunting during the winter. Each band had their own fishing and hunting grounds.

Below: The remains of a New Hampshire native's canoe

Passaconaway's Magic

Passaconaway was the leader of the Pennacook at the time the first English settlers arrived in New Hampshire. Most Native American leaders were respected for their skills as warriors and their ability to get along with people. The leaders consulted sorcerers, people who had supernatural powers, on matters concerning the spirit world. Passaconaway was unusual because his people believed he had supernatural powers in addition to fighting and leadership skills.

Passaconaway, sachem of the Pennacook, was already considered an old man when the English first encountered him. He was probably about 60 years old at the time.

Passaconaway's people reported that their leader could turn himself into a pillar of flame, make water burn, and cause trees to dance and rocks to move by themselves through the air. Nevertheless, Passaconaway believed that the Pennacooks could live peacefully with the English and treated them as friends. He invited the Massachusetts minister John Eliot to visit and preach to his village, saying of Christianity, "we know not what is within. It may be excellent or it may be nothing."

When, as an old man of nearly 100, Passaconaway handed over the leadership of the Pennacooks to his son Wonalancet in 1660, some of his people blamed him for the loss of their land to the English. Passaconaway said that he had tried magic against the English, but that the English had been too powerful. The dying chief was said to have told his son that the English god was greater than the Indian gods. Passaconaway lived to be more than 100 years old, on a tract of land granted to him by the English. Wonalancet converted to Christianity after his father's death.

3.
FISH FOR THE TAKING

David Thomson received a grant of 6,000 acres from the Council of New England. In 1623 he claimed a site at the mouth of the Piscataqua River—near present-day Rye—and named it Pannaway. The Hilton brothers received a grant of 25 square miles for a settlement located eight miles upstream, and that became Dover. Another settlement, called Strawberry Bank, was established by the company at the site of present day Portsmouth. Walter Neale was to serve as the governor of the company settlements and lead the search for the Lake of the Iroquois.

The early settlers traded with the Native Americans, offering clothing, blankets, pots, axes, and knives in exchange for furs. The colonists also caught and dried fish, and cut down tall trees and shipped lumber back to England. Faced with the hard work of survival, they had little time for producing surplus goods for the investors.

However much the settlers sent back to England, the investors were not satisfied. They had expected that this

New Hampshire's fast-flowing rivers powered sawmills to cut trees into lumber. The lumber then had to be shaped with hand tools.

land which they had never seen would easily yield up its riches to the settlers. The settlers wrote asking the Company to send more food and tools, and—most of all—more men to help with the work. Employee Ambrose Gibbins wrote from New Hampshire, "A **plantation** must be furnished with cattle and good hired hands and necessaries for them." Captain Mason wrote to the colony, "I have [spent] a great deal of money in the plantation, and never received one penny; but hope, if there were once a discovery of the lakes, that I should … be reimbursed … ."

When Mason and Gorges divided up their land in 1629, they could not have predicted that Maine would soon become a territory of Massachusetts and remain so until 1820.

One of the investors, Christopher Levett, visited the settlements in 1624 and provided a more balanced view when he reported to his associates in England: "I will not tell you that you may smell the corn fields before you see the land … nor will the deer come when they are called or stand still and look on a man until he shoots him … nor the fish leap into the kettle … but certainly, there is fowl, deer, and fish enough for the taking … ."

Ferdinando Gorges sent his son Robert to serve as governor-general of the settlements. By the time Robert arrived at Pannaway, he found a letter from his father telling him he had no more money to support the settlements.

In 1629, having failed to realize their dream of riches, Mason and Gorges dissolved the Laconia Company and split the territory between them. Mason kept the portion that he named New Hampshire, after his home county in England. Gorges's part became Maine. The settlers clinging to the New Hampshire shore would receive nothing more from the Company.

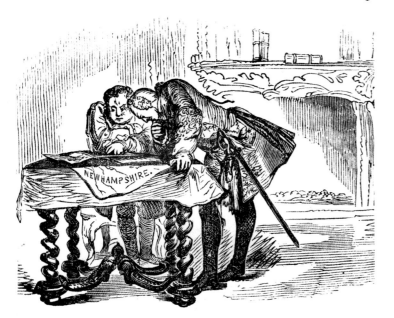

PLANTATION: COLONY OR NEWLY PLANTED SETTLEMENT

PURITAN: PROTESTANT WHO WANTED THE CHURCH OF ENGLAND TO PRACTICE A MORE "PURE" FORM OF CHRISTIANITY

ARRIVALS FROM MASSACHUSETTS

Also in 1629, the king gave a patent to a group of **Puritans**—members of a religious group that wanted to practice a more "pure" form of Christianity than that of the Church of England—for a colony on Massachusetts Bay. The new patent included some of the land that had previously been granted to Mason and Gorges. Gorges

The Puritans of Massachusetts Bay Colony

Boston, Massachusetts, was the center of Puritan government and society in America.

In England during the early 1600s, a group of Christians called themselves Puritans because they wanted to purify the Church of England, or Anglican church. Puritans believed that the Church of England included too many sinners, so they wanted to purify the church by expelling sinners. The Puritans also wanted individual churches to have the power to control their own membership, and the members, in turn, to be able to control their local leaders. In this way the Puritan church would consist only of true believers. Puritans wanted to purify the church from within. They believed that it was their Christian duty to support the church while they worked to reform it.

In 1630, John Winthrop and about 1,000 English Puritans came to Massachusetts to settle around Boston Bay. Winthrop believed he could better help purify the church in America than in England. Winthrop expected his Puritan colony to be an example to the world, writing, "We shall be a city upon a hill, the eyes of all people upon us." The Puritans arrived with their own charter and called their new land the Massachusetts Bay Colony.

The Massachusetts Bay Colony grew rapidly. By 1635, about 2,000 immigrants were coming to the colony each year and most of them were Puritans. The newcomers settled all along the Atlantic coast from Maine to Long Island. Under Governor Winthrop's leadership, the Puritans organized an efficient government that included courts, police, and tax collectors.

The Puritans believed that only devout churchgoers were suitable for leadership positions in their colony, and they did not tolerate people who disagreed with them. Puritan control of the Massachusetts Bay Colony extended into many aspects of life. The General Court set wages and prices of merchandise, made rules about how to dress, and told people where and with whom they could live. The goal of such laws was to create a stable Christian society that remained true to Puritan ideals. The effort pleased the most devout Puritans. It made life uncomfortable for most everyone else. Increasing numbers of colonists began to view the Puritan laws as too restrictive and looked for another place to settle.

TITLE: CLAIM TO A PIECE OF PROPERTY

Maple ashes were used to make potash, which was much in demand to make medicine, soap, fertilizer, and a fire extinguishing compound. Potash received its name from the way it was made by boiling ashes in huge pots.

argued that since the planned Bay Colony was in Council of New England territory, it should be under the Council's control. Eventually, a special panel was appointed to study the matter, and it concluded that Massachusetts Bay Colony should remain a separate royal colony, leaving Gorges with only his **title** to Maine.

The Hiltons, meanwhile, sold most of their land grant to a group of Massachusetts Puritans, and in that way made their settlement the only one to actually make a profit. John Mason died in 1635, leaving the grant to his grandsons. This led to more than 100 years of legal conflict over the ownership of substantial parcels of New Hampshire land. Some settlers had received their land grants from agents of the Laconia Company, and others from the heirs of John Mason. Others still simply settled where they pleased. All groups feared that, as more settlers came from Massachusetts, the Massachusetts authorities might claim to their land at any time.

HERESY: BELIEF THAT IS
DENOUNCED BY ONE'S
CHURCH

When a group of Massachusetts Puritans bought land at Dover from one of the earliest settlers, they quickly built a meeting house with a protective fence around it and hired a minister.

The settlers sent to New Hampshire by the Laconia Company learned for certain that they were on their own when they received letters from the investors in England refusing to send more supplies. In addition, men began arriving from the Massachusetts Bay Colony to claim the land around their small settlements. However, the New Hampshire settlements at Strawberry Bank and on the Isles of Shoals continued to grow. They attracted tough and independent-minded people from the inland settlements, England, and Massachusetts Bay who hoped to make a good living by fishing. Some of the people who migrated north from Massachusetts Bay were loyal to the Massachusetts government but looking for money-making opportunities. Many, however, wanted to escape the Bay Colony's strict Puritan government. The Puritans also expelled people who disagreed with them.

In 1638, the Bay Colony banished Reverend John Wheelwright and his congregation, calling them Antinomians. Antinomians believed that religious people could have a direct relationship with God. The Puritans of Massachusetts considered these beliefs to be **heresy**. Wheelwright's group founded the town of Exeter and set up their own town government. Massachusetts authorities, concerned that New Hampshire would

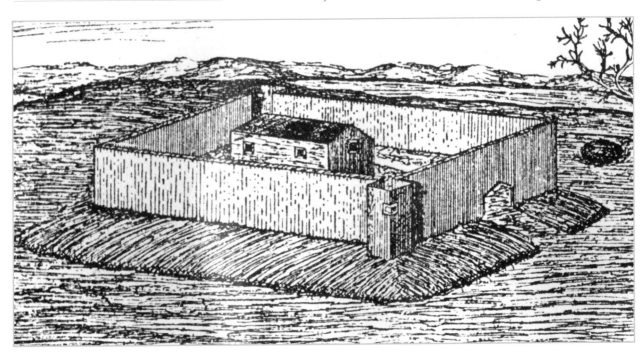

become a refuge for all sorts of undesirable people, complained that the New Hampshire settlers should not have allowed Wheelwright's group to settle among them. The complaints fell on deaf ears, as most New Hampshire settlers were Anglicans who had no love for Puritans.

By 1640, about a thousand English people lived in New Hampshire, and more than half of them had moved there from Massachusetts Bay Colony. New Hampshire soon had four towns: Portsmouth and Dover, settled by fishermen and lumbermen, and Exeter and Hampton, settled by religious groups, most of whose members were farmers. The New Hampshire townspeople asked the Massachusetts Bay government to take their towns under

Building a new town was a cooperative effort for Puritan settlers.

From its beginnings as a fishing village called Strawberry Bank, the growing town was officially renamed Portsmouth in 1653.

Bay Colony authority, and by 1651, Massachusetts had extended its authority over all New Hampshire towns. However, each town still had its own local government and a great deal of control over its own affairs.

The people of England had recently fought a civil war, which ended with the execution of King Charles I in 1649 and the establishment of a Puritan government under Oliver Cromwell. The Puritans of New England had welcomed the new government. They were less pleased, however, when the dead king's son resumed the English throne in 1660 as King Charles II.

Charles II willingly accepted a suggestion by Robert Mason, the grandson of the late Captain John Mason, to investigate the Massachusetts takeover of New Hampshire. In 1664, the king appointed a special commission to visit New England. The king's commissioners planned to reduce the power of Massachusetts by separating New Hampshire from it, but the Puritans living in New Hampshire wished to remain under the Massachusetts government. A disastrous fire in London and the outbreak of war between England and the Netherlands temporarily put a stop to the planned separation.

THE END OF PEACE

As ever increasing numbers of English colonists settled New England, the native peoples saw that their way of life was in peril. White settlements surrounded many Native American villages. As the English settlers cleared woodlands to create fields and sell lumber, the wild game retreated inland, and the Native Americans had to travel farther and farther to have successful hunts. English sawmills and dams on the rivers destroyed populations of salmon and other freshwater fish. English livestock trampled and ate the Native Americans' corn crops.

The Wampanoag people had lived in peace with the English ever since 1620 when their leader, Massasoit, made a treaty of friendship with the Pilgrims in Massachusetts. Massasoit's son, Metacom, called King Philip by the English, saw that he was losing control of his lands and his power. As the English forced him to give up more and more land, Metacom organized a Native American alliance to resist English expansion.

In June 1675, a war broke out between the Wampanoags and the English who lived in Massachusetts. The war began with the Native Americans making surprise attacks on isolated **frontier** settlements. They succeeded in destroying numerous villages. In New Hampshire, they attacked a settlement near the site of present-day Durham, killing and capturing English men, women, and children

English colonists taken captive by Native Americans faced an uncertain fate. They might be killed, forced to work, or returned to their people in exchange for a ransom payment. Some captive children were adopted by Native Americans and stayed with them for so many years that they forgot how to speak English.

ALLIES: PEOPLE OR NATIONS
WHO HAVE AGREED TO
COOPERATE, OR TO FIGHT
ON THE SAME SIDE IN A WAR

MILITIA: GROUP OF
CITIZENS NOT NORMALLY
PART OF THE ARMY WHO
JOIN TOGETHER TO
DEFEND THEIR LAND
IN AN EMERGENCY

and burning houses. This attack signaled the beginning of the so-called King Philip's War and the end of the colonists' previously peaceful lives in New Hampshire.

The New England colonies, with the exception of Rhode Island, united to fight Metacom. Some groups of Native Americans allied themselves with Metacom, others with the English. Most of the important battles of the war took place outside of New Hampshire. In December 1675, the English inflicted a major defeat on the Native Americans during a bloody battle in Rhode Island. During the winter, the surviving Native Americans continued to raid throughout New England. When spring came, most Native American fighting men had to concentrate on hunting and fishing in order to help feed their families. The English had greater resources to support a war and so they kept hunting down the enemy. By June, Massachusetts leaders offered to spare any Native American who surrendered. Hundreds took advantage of this offer. However, the Native Americans had killed one out of every sixteen English fighting men.

All that remained was to track down Metacom himself. A group of whites and their native **allies** found and killed him on August 12, 1676. Although some fighting continued for another two years, Metacom's death marked the end of the greatest—but not the last—military challenge the Native Americans ever mounted against New England.

Before and during King Philip's War in New Hampshire, most of the Pennacook, under the leadership of Passaconaway's son, Wonalancet, remained friendly with the English. After the war ended, the Pennacook permitted refugee Nipmuc, who had fought against the English, to stay with them. Major Richard Waldron, the New Hampshire **militia** commander, invited a group of Pennacook and Nipmuc to visit him. Waldron then seized the Nipmucs and sold them into slavery. Waldron's trick violated the rules of hospitality and humiliated the Pennacook. Many Pennacook then gave up on the idea of peaceful coexistence with the English and abandoned their homeland for Maine. But some remained, and waited for the chance to take revenge. Thirteen years later they seized the moment.

4.
LIFE AND DEATH IN THE ROYAL COLONY

England and the Netherlands finally made peace in 1674 after years of fighting. At Robert Mason's urging, King Charles II again turned his attention to the colonies and Massachusetts's continued hold on New Hampshire. His agents found people in New Hampshire even less willing to separate from Massachusetts. King Philip's war had drawn the two neighbors closer as they fought together to defend their frontier.

When King Charles II was restored to the English throne after the fall of the Puritan Commonwealth, Massachusetts ordered the New Hampshire settlements not to cooperate with visiting royal officials.

FREEMAN: MAN WHO WAS WHITE AND AT LEAST 21 YEARS OLD, AND WHO HAD THE RIGHT TO VOTE OR HOLD OFFICE

ACT: LAW, SO CALLED BECAUSE IT IS MADE BY AN ACT OF GOVERNMENT

The oldest building still standing in Portsmouth was built in 1664.

However, Massachusetts authorities angered English officials by refusing to cooperate with royal officials. English authorities threatened to take over Massachusetts as a royal colony, but in the end decided simply to proceed with their plans to give New Hampshire a separate government from that of Massachusetts. New Hampshire would have its own royal governor, who would officially be the lieutenant-governor of Massachusetts. The decision took effect in 1680. New Hampshire's first years as a royal colony proved to be difficult.

The colony's approximately 2,000 inhabitants were to be ruled by an appointed governor and his council and an assembly elected by the **freemen** in each town. Most of the new government officials—Puritan church members—supported the same laws that had existed under Massachusetts authority. One of the first **acts** of the New Hampshire assembly was to deny Mason the right to collect rent on the land once held by his grandfather. In 1682, Edward Cranfield, the first governor, arrived and

overturned everything that had been done in the past two years. He removed most of the government from office and replaced them with men of his choosing, restored Mason's right to collect rent, and ordered the Puritans to open church membership to non-Puritans.

Cranfield's main goal, under instructions from the crown, was to make the people of New Hampshire obey English laws, especially the laws governing shipping and trade. Merchants and shippers had been ignoring the laws requiring them to pay **duties** on imported goods, but Cranfield instituted searches of all vessels. Many of the people of New Hampshire simply refused to obey. They continued smuggling and refused to pay all taxes and rents. Gangs beat up government officials and threatened to beat the governor. Nearly half the adult men in New Hampshire signed a formal complaint to London. Fearing for his safety at the hands of what he called "these unreasonable people," Cranfield fled to Boston in 1684.

> DUTIES: TAXES COLLECTED ON GOODS BROUGHT INTO A COUNTRY

The defiance of English laws by the New England colonies, especially Massachusetts, gave the new king of England, James II, a reason to take greater control of the colonies. In 1685, the king merged Massachusetts Bay, Plymouth, New Hampshire, and Maine (a province of Massachusetts) into a single colony called the Dominion of New England, with Sir Edmund Andros as the royal governor. Rhode Island and Connecticut were the next to be taken over, followed by New Jersey and New York.

Governor Edmund Andros controlled the Dominion from his offices in Boston. As time passed, the governor became so unpopular that when news arrived in 1689 of James II being forced from the throne in England, a group of armed civilians rebelled and captured Andros. The new king, William III, having just declared war on France, permitted the colonies to resume governing themselves, and New Hampshire again became a colony separate from Massachusetts. King William's War was to last nine years. The war began in Europe, but it laid waste to the New Hampshire frontier.

DEATH ON THE FRONTIER

England and France were great rivals who, throughout their history, had often resorted to war to resolve disagreements. Even during peaceful times they competed fiercely. When **British** and French settlers came to North America, they brought their conflict with them. New France lay to the north of New England, in present-day Canada. However, Native American country lay between the English and French colonies, and many native peoples had become allies of the French, including the Abenaki of Maine and New Hampshire. As the 1600s drew to a close, the French in North America and their Native American allies grew in numbers and strength, and frontier New Englanders lived in fear of attack. As Puritans and **Protestants**, they worried, with good reason, that Catholic missionaries from France would convert the native peoples and stir them up to fight a religious war.

Meanwhile, in 1688 England and France went to war with one another in Europe. The war continued until 1697. This war, and another war that raged from 1701 to 1714, spilled over into the American colonies. Throughout those years, French and Native American forces attacked New England settlements, and New England forces and their Native American allies attacked French settlements in a never-ending cycle of attacks and revenge. The outbreak of war gave the offended Pennacook their long-awaited chance to take revenge on Richard Waldron for his betrayal.

Above: The official seal of the colony of New Hampshire, 1692, reads "The Seal of Our Province of New Hampshire in New England." After the Dominion of New England came to an end, New Hampshire again became a separate colony.

BRITISH: THE NATIONALITY OF A PERSON BORN IN GREAT BRITAIN; PEOPLE BORN IN ENGLAND ARE CALLED "ENGLISH".

Opposite: Governor Andros in Boston, Massachusetts. Andros did not have the time to interfere in New Hampshire government because the uncooperative people of Massachusetts kept him fully occupied.

In 1689, the Pennacook and Abenaki launched several surprise attacks on frontier settlements, many of them in New Hampshire. Prominent among the targeted settlements was that of Richard Waldron near Dover. After years of peace, the unsuspecting colonists gave shelter to two Native American women who asked to stay the night in Waldron's fortified settlement. After the colonists went to sleep, the women opened the doors to the attackers. The attackers tortured Waldron to death, killed 22 others, and captured 29. Similar attacks occurred at other settlements. Exeter and Portsmouth each endured attacks. The fighting ceased during the brief interval between the end of King William's War in 1697 and the outbreak of Queen Anne's War in 1701.

By the time the Native Americans attacked Hampton in 1703, New Hampshire had organized a system of small forts for defense and mounted pre-emptive attacks on native villages in Maine. Still, the Native Americans made several raids during the years of Queen Anne's War,

During the wars between the English colonists and the native peoples, many captives suffered extremely cruel treatment.

including an unsuccessful attempt to kill the son of the hated Richard Waldron. In 1713, the English and the Native Americans of New Hampshire signed a peace treaty at Portsmouth. Although the two wars had frightened colonists into abandoning several New Hampshire settlements, they severely reduced the Native American population. During the 1600s, European diseases may have killed nineteen out of twenty Native Americans in New Hampshire. The drawn-out years of warfare completed their destruction. Fewer than 100 of the once numerous Pennacook remained.

When Queen Anne's War ended in Europe, the French gave up their possessions of Newfoundland and Nova Scotia to the British. However, France still held a sizeable part of Canada bordering New England.

The World at War

During the colonial period in North America, war between England and other European powers was a regular occurrence. Between 1652 and 1674, England fought three wars with the Netherlands. Then in 1688, England began the first of four wars against France. During each of these wars, battles took place in Europe, at sea, and in the American colonies held by each of the warring European powers.

From 1688 to 1697, England and the Netherlands, formerly enemies, joined together to fight against France. This war was called the War of the Grand Alliance or the Nine Years' War in Europe. In America it was called King William's War, and battles took place in New York, New England, and Canada.

From 1701 to 1714, England fought France and Spain in the War of the Spanish Succession. In America, the war was called Queen Anne's War, and fighting took place in Canada, New England, South Carolina, and Florida.

From 1740 to 1748, Great Britain fought Spain, France, and other European powers in the War of the Austrian Succession. The war had begun in Europe in 1740, but France did not enter the war until 1744, when it declared war on Britain and attacked the British-held town of Annapolis Royal, Nova Scotia. In America, the war was called King George's War, and most of the battles took place in Nova Scotia. French and Native American raiders also attacked settlements in Maine.

The so-called Seven Years' War between France and Great Britain took place between 1754 and 1763. In America it was called the French and Indian War. Battles took place from Pennsylvania to Canada. Many American military men learned about war during the French and Indian War. They used this experience when they fought the British in the Revolutionary War.

5.
YEARS OF GROWTH

In 1717, the king of **Great Britain**, George I, appointed John Wentworth the lieutenant-governor of Massachusetts, which meant that he was the governor in charge of New Hampshire. Wentworth was a wealthy merchant from Exeter and had served on the New Hampshire council for many years. As governor he faced significant problems, including Native American raids and disputes with Massachusetts over its boundary line. By the time Wentworth died in 1730, the colony had attracted many new settlers and driven most of the Native Americans from its territory.

Beginning in 1719, Scotch-Irish Presbyterians began settling in New Hampshire. They were not Irish, but actually Scottish people who had lived in Ulster, Northern Ireland. Driven from Ireland by poverty, they wanted a chance to

In 1718, 300 Scottish people living in Ulster, Northern Ireland, signed a petition asking for permission to purchase land in New England. Many of them ended up in New Hampshire.

The trees of New Hampshire provided plentiful raw materials for building ships.

New England shipbuilding boomed in the 1700s. New Hampshire supplied more than masts and planks. The coastal area also had sailmakers and ropewalks (below), which produced ropes for sailing ships.

own land. Those who came to Massachusetts found that the Puritans did not welcome them, so many moved on to New Hampshire. A group of Scotch-Irish people founded the town of Londonderry. Over the next ten years, about a thousand Scotch-Irish came to New Hampshire.

Another group of immigrants came from Great Britain. As New England developed its own shipbuilding industry, New England shipyards began winning customers away from British shipyards, and by the 1720s, many British shipwrights and carpenters moved to New England.

As cold as the climate was, land was still available in New Hampshire long after the best land had been occupied in the rest of New England. Much of New Hampshire's available land lay along rivers and still had many valuable trees on it.

Trees and Ships

New Hampshire had two essential ingredients for a profitable lumber industry: plentiful timber and briskly flowing rivers for powering sawmills. Ninety sawmills were operating in New Hampshire by 1700. New Hampshire trees were cut up to make such products as lumber for buildings, barrel staves, and shingles, which were exported both to the other colonies and to the West Indies. However, New Hampshire's largest trees were most in demand for shipbuilding, especially the giant white pine trees, which grew tall and straight. These trees were 500 to 1,000 years old and close to 200 feet tall. They ranged from three to six feet in diameter at the base. No such trees existed in Great Britain.

The British Royal Navy had a great and continuing need for trees suitable to make masts for sailing ships, and searched for them around the world. American pines were known to make stronger masts than the Norwegian pines the navy had been using.

Portsmouth became a center of the mast trade, which made up about 10 percent of New Hampshire's lumber earnings. A single mast tree exported to England was worth a great deal of money, and white pines made the most profit for New Hampshire lumber merchants.

Each great mast tree was cut down by two axemen working together. They aimed to drop the tree with its base pointing toward the seacoast and prepared a bed of brush to cushion its fall. Winter was the best time to cut because the snow provided a cushion for the falling tree and made it easier to drag the tree to the nearest river. As many as 50 pairs of oxen might be needed to drag the tree to the water on a special sled. Many oxen died of exhaustion from dragging trees. By 1700, mast trees could be found no closer than 20 miles inland. By 1750 they had almost all been cut down.

Mast trees were brought to mast houses, where they were stripped of bark, shaped by skilled workers, and cut to the right length. A specialized type of vessel called a "mast ship" was required to carry the great pine trunks across the Atlantic Ocean. A loaded mast ship, holding as many as 100 masts, was heavy and hard to handle in a storm. Fearing piracy of such extremely valuable cargo, such ships sometimes sailed with armed escorts. Ten mast ships a year left Portsmouth during the height of the trade.

From the early 1700s, Britain tried to control New Hampshire's dwindling supply of great trees by marking them and prohibiting anyone from cutting them down without a license. The colonists heartily resented this attempt to deprive them of free use of their resources, and many people cut down marked trees when they could do so without being caught.

Above: The lumber industry provided wood for barrel staves. Barrels were in great demand as containers for storing and shipping goods ranging from cider to whale oil.

Right: Teams of oxen were worked year-round to remove felled trees from the forests.

As English settlements expanded northward, war again broke out in 1722 between the English and the Abenakis who had been armed by the French. In 1724, Massachusetts and New Hampshire decided to end Abenaki raids for good by sending 200 militia to attack the central Abenaki village in nearby Maine. This attack killed at least eighty Abenakis. The colonial governments then offered to pay generous bounties for Native American scalps. The resulting bloodshed convinced the surviving Native Americans to migrate across the St. Lawrence River into Canada. By 1730, virtually no Native Americans remained in New Hampshire.

During the 1730s, New Hampshire and Massachusetts argued over their shared border. In 1740, King George II set the boundary in a way that gave New Hampshire a lot of new territory at the expense of Massachusetts. The colony's population grew from 10,000 to more than 20,000 between 1730 and 1740.

By 1741, New Hampshire had grown enough to have an entirely separate government from Massachusetts. One of John Wentworth's sixteen children, Benning Wentworth, was appointed to be the first full governor—not lieutenant-governor—of New Hampshire. He kept the

Governor Benning Wentworth's large, elegant home in Portsmouth also served as the meeting place of New Hampshire's governing council.

job for 25 years. During Wentworth's administration, Portsmouth became a prosperous and stylish colonial capital with elegant homes.

Wentworth also expanded New Hampshire's territory by granting large tracts of land on the western side of the Connecticut River, in what later became Vermont. He did this over the objections of New York, which also claimed the land and made land grants to its people. About 20,000 people from both colonies settled in Vermont before the Revolution, and sometimes had armed conflicts over possession of land.

When war again broke out between France and Great Britain (King George's War, 1744–1748), Wentworth joined the Massachusetts governor in planning a surprise attack to capture the French fortress of Louisbourg, on Cape Breton Island at the eastern end of Nova Scotia. New Englanders were concerned that the French were competing with them for control of the North Atlantic fishing grounds, and that they were continuing to stir up the native peoples against the British colonists.

In 1745, New Hampshire militia joined with militia from the rest of New England, and the 4,000-man force, under the leadership of William Pepperell of Maine, captured the fortress after a long siege that used up 9,000 cannonballs. The victorious New Englanders were disgusted when Louisbourg became a bargaining chip in peace negotiations and was returned to France at the war's end in 1748. Only six more years would pass before France and Great Britain went to war for the fourth time.

THE FRENCH AND INDIAN WAR

In spite of the defeats France had recently suffered at the hands of the British, French explorers claimed all of North America from the Allegheny Mountains to the Rocky Mountains and from Canada to Mexico. Few French people settled in the vast area south of Canada. Instead, French traders followed waterways to hunt and trap and to trade with Native Americans. British traders also traveled westward to the far side of the Allegheny Mountains

Benning Wentworth (above) was a poor man when he became governor of New Hampshire, but he grew wealthy while in office. All five of his sons died in childhood. He was succeeded as governor in 1767 by his nephew, John Wentworth, who remained as governor until the beginning of the Revolutionary War.

The "New Hampshire Grants," or Vermont

During the 1740s and 1750s, colonists from Massachusetts and Connecticut who were seeking unoccupied land moved into the area north of Massachusetts and west of the Connecticut River. This area eventually became the present-day state of Vermont, named after the French words for the Green Mountains. The British king, George II, had placed much of the land under the control of New Hampshire in 1740. The new settlers applied to New Hampshire for land grants, so the area came to be called the "New Hampshire Grants."

The next British king, George III, declared in 1764 that New Hampshire ended at the Connecticut River, putting Vermont in the hands of the colony of New York. The people living in the nearly 100 small towns of the New Hampshire Grants were angry at being placed under the control of New York. Rather than rejoin New Hampshire, however, in 1777 the people of Vermont declared themselves independent of New York.

Then, three dozen towns on the New Hampshire side of the Connecticut River threatened to withdraw permanently from New Hampshire, now a state, and join Vermont. The towns' inhabitants believed that the New Hampshire government favored the coastal population and did not represent them. The New Hampshire representatives changed parts of the state constitution in order to persuade the runaway towns to return.

Vermont never received a charter as a royal colony. Instead, after the American Revolution in 1791 Vermont became the fourteenth state.

Ethan Allen moved to the so-called New Hampshire Grants when he was about 30 years old. In 1770, he became the commander of the "Green Mountain Boys," organized to fight New York's claim to the territory. Some people considered Allen's force no better than a mob, and New York's governor offered a reward for his capture. In 1775, Allen heard about the Battle of Lexington and decided on his own to lead his Green Mountain Boys into New York to capture Fort Ticonderoga from the British. Allen's men surprised the fort's commander and took the fort without firing a shot.

to trade with the native peoples of the Ohio River valley. France wanted to keep control of the Ohio country, but British colonists wanted to expand westward.

Concerned about French maneuvers in the west, New Hampshire joined representatives from the other New England colonies, Pennsylvania, Maryland, and the Iroquois peoples of New York in Albany in June 1754 to discuss cooperation against the French. The Albany Congress also discussed a bold plan for a union among the colonies, but in the end, the colonies feared that they would lose control over their own affairs, and the British government feared it would lose control over the colonies.

A month later, a new war between the French and the British began on disputed land near modern day Pittsburgh, Pennsylvania, with a small battle between Virginia militia and French soldiers. This battle to control the Ohio River valley erupted into a long and deadly conflict. In Europe the war became known as the Seven Years' War. Americans called it the French and Indian War.

George Washington's first military experience was in the French and Indian War. He is shown here retreating from Fort Necessity after his surrender to the French in 1754.

During the previous war, New Hampshire had built a chain of forts to defend its frontier from attack. New Hampshire militiamen again manned these forts to defend the frontier, and sent several hundred men to fight the enemy in New York and other parts of New England. Nearly a thousand New Hampshire militiamen took part in the French and Indian War, among them a group called Rogers's Rangers, commanded by Captain Robert Rogers. New Hampshire militia also helped capture Crown Point in New York and built an 87-mile military road across the Green Mountains of Vermont.

The French and Indian War ended with the defeat of

A Rogers' Ranger in winter dress. Rangers were able to move quickly and quietly through the country-side. They were valued for their ability to conduct raids and reconnaissance.

the French in 1759. After France and Great Britain made peace in 1763, Canada became another British colony.

NEW HAMPSHIRE BETWEEN TWO WARS

At the end of the French and Indian War, New Hampshire of the 1760s was home to a diverse population. Its borders encompassed people of different religions and levels of wealth. The majority of the people belonged to the **Congregational** church, founded by the Puritans. Of the 118 churches in New Hampshire, 84 of them were Congregationalist. Scotch-Irish people belonged to the Presbyterian church. **Anglicans** and Quakers also lived in

CONGREGATIONAL: CHURCH ORGANIZED BY PURITANS, BASED ON THE IDEA THAT EACH CONGREGATION GOVERNED ITSELF WITHOUT INTERFERENCE FROM A CENTRAL AUTHORITY

ANGLICAN: CHURCH OF ENGLAND, A PROTESTANT CHURCH AND THE STATE CHURCH OF ENGLAND

In 1759, Robert Rogers and his Rangers burned a Native American village in Canada and slaughtered the inhabitants.

the colony. All residents of New Hampshire were required by law to pay taxes and support a church, but they could choose which church to support.

The end of the war and the departure of the French authorities from Canada encouraged new immigrants to flock to the region. New Hampshire soon had more than 150 towns, and the colony's population grew from 50,000 to 75,000 during the decade before the beginning of the

Main Picture: Portsmouth in the 1770s

Right: Although most of New Hampshire's churches were Puritan, other churches were tolerated. Many Puritans and Presbyterians supported the idea of independence from Great Britain, while Anglicans remained loyal to Britain, and Quakers opposed all war.

A New Hampshire farm. The cold climate of New Hampshire made it impossible to grow some of the crops familiar to British people, but apple and pear trees did especially well.

Revolution. The major seaport, Portsmouth, had a population of close to 5,000.

In spite of the cold climate and short growing season, the majority of New Hampshire colonists engaged in farming. In addition to raising crops and animals for food, many worked at businesses and trades. For example, Samuel Lane of Stratham, New Hampshire, worked at farming, tanning leather, making shoes, and surveying land. The grandson of people who had moved to Hampton, New Hampshire, from Boston in 1686, Lane

started supporting himself in 1739 at the age of 21.

"Money being scarce, it was difficult to get money for my work: and the best method I could think of was, to make shoes & some fishing boots … and my practice was when I had got a little cargo made, to carry them over to the [Isles of] Shoals; and when I could not get money for them, I would sell them for oil, blubber, & fish … I have draw'd off 2 barrels of oil in a fall; & sold it for corn; then I would endeavor to turn the corn into money. … Sometimes I took boards & shingles & nails for my work."

Left: New Hampshire printed paper money, but it was always in short supply. People usually bartered, exchanging their labor or goods they had produced for other goods they needed.

Below: In 1760, Samuel Lane, a New Hampshire farmer and shoemaker, wrote, "This week past my 2 sons Sam in the 14th and Joshua in the 12th year of their ages made 14 pair of women's pumps [shoes]."

Above: People used hand tools to make furniture and household objects out of such woods as birch, maple, cherry, and pine.

Left: Whole families gathered in their living rooms during the winters, when little could be done outdoors, and worked at making items for their own use or for sale.

Lane soon prospered, and could boast of his own home and land, a growing family, and a successful business.

However, the weather often turned against New Hampshire's farmers. In some years, early frosts, even in early August, ruined food crops. Crop failures could be followed by a winter of exceptionally deep snows, so that farmers with nothing to feed their livestock could not put them out to graze. When livestock starved, farmers could not plow their fields. Droughts and insects sometimes destroyed crops as well. In one bad year, 1762, Samuel Lane wrote, "by the month of Febr. there was scarcely any [corn] to be bought, and so many people coming about after it, begging & pleading for it, almost in a starving condition ... that those people amongst us, that had corn sufficient for their own families, could not keep it; but were obliged in duty to hearken to the cries of those that had none." Yet two years later, Lane could report "a comfortable winter & provisions plenty."

6.
REVOLUTION

On the day before the Stamp Act took effect, the *New Hampshire Gazette* published this issue lamenting the loss of liberty. The Portsmouth Sons of Liberty, however, considered the *New Hampshire Gazette* to be too conservative and pro-British, so they formed an alternative paper.

After the war ended, British leaders concluded that the American colonies had not helped as much as they should have. Moreover, the British government still needed to provide about 10,000 soldiers to defend the colonies. This was a heavy expense. Never before had the British **Parliament** set taxes on American citizens. This changed in 1764. To help pay for the cost of defending the colonies, Parliament passed a law to raise money from the American colonies themselves. This law was the Sugar Act. The Sugar Act imposed a tax on imports or exports. Such taxes are called duties. The Sugar Act placed duties on refined sugar as well as other trade goods and provided for strict enforcement and collection procedures. The Sugar Act was the first in a series of decisions made by the British Parliament that led to the American Revolution.

Next, in 1765 Parliament passed the Stamp Act. Under the Stamp Act, colonists had to pay to have most documents stamped, or else risk arrest. Even newspapers had to have stamps. The Stamp Act affected colonists of all social classes. Resistance grew, and groups calling themselves the Sons of Liberty formed throughout the colonies. A group in Portsmouth organized a local Sons of Liberty, which held protests and forced the local stamp agent to resign. New Hampshire's towns began electing representatives to the assembly who did not want to cooperate with British tax laws.

The outcry in America persuaded Parliament to repeal the Stamp Act in 1766, but King George III insisted that Great Britain's Parliament still had the right to make laws for the colonies and collect taxes. The following year, Parliament passed a new set of laws taxing even more products, and angered more colonists. Protesters throughout the colonies opposed British laws by forming Committees of Correspondence. By writing letters, the Committees kept one another informed and made plans for the colonies to cooperate. The Committees organized a **boycott** of all trade with Great Britain, which the New Hampshire assembly voted to join. The governor ordered one of his appointees to intercept the assembly's correspondence with the other colonies, and thus prevented New Hampshire from taking part in the boycott. However, the boycott convinced the British to

King George III believed that if he gave in to the demands of American patriots, Great Britain's other colonies would rebel.

Twelve days after the raid on Fort William and Mary, Governor Wentworth issued a proclamation calling for all citizens to help track down the raiders and the stolen armaments.

Province of NEW-HAMPSHIRE

A PROCLAMATION,
BY THE GOVERNOR.

WHEREAS several Bodies of Men did, in the Day Time of the 14th, and in the Night of the 15th of this Instant December, in the most daring and rebellious Manner invest, attack, and forcibly enter into His Majesty's Castle William and Mary in this Province, and overpowering and confining the Captain and Garrison, did, besides committing many treasonable Insults and Outrages, break open the Magazine of said Castle and plunder it of above One hundred Barrels of Gunpowder, with upwards of sixty Stand of small Arms, and did also force from the Ramparts of said Castle and carry off sixteen Pieces of Cannon, and other military Stores, in open Hostility and direct Oppugnation of His Majesty's Government, and in the most atrocious Contempt of his Crown and Dignity ;----

I Do, by Advice and Consent of His Majesty's Council, issue this Proclamation, ordering and requiring, in his Majesty's Name, all Magistrates and other Officers, whether Civil or Military, as they regard their Duty to the KING and the Tenor of the Oaths they have solemnly taken and subscribed, to exert themselves in detecting and securing in some of his Majesty's Goals in this province the said Offenders, in Order to their being brought to condign punishment ; And from Motives of Duty to the King and Regard to the Welfare of the good People of this Province : I do in the most earnest and solemn Manner, exhort and injoin you, his Majesty's liege Subjects of this Government, to beware of suffering yourselves to be seduced by the false Arts or Menaces of abandoned Men, to abet, protect, or screen from Justice any of the said high handed Offenders, or to withhold or secrete his Majesty's Munition forcibly taken from his Castle ; but that each and every of you will use your utmost Endeavours to detect and discover the Perpetrators of these Crimes to the civil Magistrate, and assist in securing and bringing them to Justice, and in recovering the King's Munition ; This Injunction it is my bounden Duty to lay strictly upon you, and to require your Obedience thereto, as you value individually your Faith and Allegiance to his Majesty, as you wish to preserve that Reputation to the Province in general ; and as you would avert the dreadful but most certain Consequences of a contrary Conduct to yourselves and Posterity.

GIVEN at the Council-Chamber in Portsmouth, the 26th Day of December, in the 15th Year of the Reign of our Sovereign Lord GEORGE the Third, by the Grace of GOD, of Great-Britain, France and Ireland, KING, Defender of the Faith, &c. and in the Year of our Lord CHRIST, 1774.

By His EXCELLENCY's Command, with Advice of Council.
J. WENTWORTH.

Theodore Atkinson, Secry.

GOD SAVE THE KING.

repeal most taxes by 1770, and normal trade resumed between Britain and the colonies.

Then Parliament passed a law that gave one British tea seller, the struggling East India Company, special treatment. The East India Company was given a **monopoly** in the colonies, so that it could sell its tea more cheaply than any other dealer. Once again, the Committees of Correspondence went to work to spread the word about the new law. The Sons of Liberty also organized actions against tea shipments. The first such action was the famous Boston Tea Party. On December 16, 1773, a group of about 150 **patriots** disguised as Mohawk Native Americans dumped a large, valuable shipment of tea into Boston Harbor.

Great Britain responded to the Boston Tea Party by closing the port of Boston and placing Massachusetts under military rule. The British goal was to teach all the colonies to submit to British rule, but Boston, the main source of trouble, was the special target. Many New Hampshire colonists had resented paying British taxes, but Britain's reaction to the Boston Tea Party stirred them to take action. Governor John Wentworth (Benning Wentworth's nephew and governor since 1767) further angered people by hiring carpenters and sending them to Boston to help build barracks for British troops. Sympathy for the patriot cause, and for their neighbors in Massachusetts, grew among the people of New Hampshire. Local Committees of Correspondence raised money to send for the relief of Boston.

Governor Wentworth dissolved the assembly, whose members increasingly supported resistance to Great Britain. The assembly met anyway in July 1774 and called for all the towns in the colony to send delegates to a convention to be held at Exeter. The first act of this convention was to choose delegates to a Continental Congress of all the colonies, which was to be held in Philadelphia in September 1774.

The First Continental Congress drew up a set of resolutions that set forth basic rights to life, liberty, property, and the rights of colonial assemblies to tax and make local laws. The First Continental Congress moved the American quarrel with Great Britain beyond taxes. In addition to tax questions, the congress questioned whether Parliament had the right to make laws for America. The delegates agreed to end all imports from Great Britain in order to pressure Parliament to accept their views. They formed a Continental Association by which every village, town, and city was to elect a committee to enforce the decrees of the Continental Congress. Finally, the delegates agreed to meet again in May 1775.

In December 1774, Paul Revere rode from Boston to Portsmouth to warn citizens that a British ship was heading their way with soldiers to build up the **garrison** at nearby Fort William and Mary. In response, 400 New Hampshire men seized the fort, confiscated the gunpowder stored there, and captured the British soldiers guarding the

GARRISON: SOLDIERS STATIONED AT A FORT TO PROTECT IT

The British surrender of Fort William & Mary

fort. Governor Wentworth ordered the militia to stop the raid, but the militia refused to obey him. By the time the British ship arrived, the fort was empty except for a few cannons without ammunition.

Wentworth fired John Sullivan, a militia officer who had led the raid on Fort William and Mary. Sullivan and other patriot officers resigned from the colonial militia and then reformed the militia in the service of the patriot cause. Militia drilled in every town, preparing to fight for independence. Their opportunity came in April 1775.

General Thomas Gage, the royal governor of Massachusetts, organized a British military force to march first to Lexington and then on to Concord to seize weapons collected by the rebellious Massachusetts militia. The British forces entered Lexington early on the morning of April 19, 1775 and encountered a small force of patriots. Which side fired the first shot is unknown. By the time the smoke cleared, the Revolutionary War had begun. The British continued on to Concord to search for hidden weapons and supplies. Meanwhile, American militia gathered from nearby towns. Fighting broke out and continued for the remainder of the day as the British retreated back to Boston.

During the course of the battle, news quickly spread, and about 1,200 New Hampshire men took up their muskets and marched toward Concord, Massachusetts, to help their neighbors resist the British forces. Over the next few days, thousands more New Hampshire patriots poured into Massachusetts and gathered on the outskirts of Boston, ready to join the fight. The New Hampshire assembly quickly voted to supply 2,000 soldiers for the Continental army.

In August 1775, Governor Wentworth and his family left New Hampshire for good on a British ship. By January 1776, New Hampshire had formed a new government with an elected house of representatives made up of members elected by each town. A Committee of Safety took the place of the governor. The new government sent three men— Josiah Bartlett, William Whipple, and Matthew Thornton—

Colonel John Stark led New Hampshire troops at the Battle of Bunker Hill. He became one of the Continental army's most successful generals. Stark had served in Rogers' Rangers during the French and Indian War.

PRIVATEER: PRIVATELY
OWNED SHIP WITH
GOVERNMENT PERMISSION
TO ATTACK THE SHIPS OF
ENEMY NATIONS DURING
WARTIME

More than 900 New Hampshire volunteers fought at the Battle of Bunker Hill on June 17, 1775.

to the second Continental Congress in Philadelphia, where they signed the Declaration of Independence in July. The representatives officially established the State of New Hampshire by September 1776.

New Hampshire prepared to defend its coast and its border with Canada from possible British attacks. An old ship was scuttled, or sunk, in the entrance of Portsmouth harbor to block British ships from entering. No fighting ever occurred on New Hampshire soil, but many **privateer**s sailed from the New Hampshire coast to attack British ships. New Hampshire shipbuilders also built ships, including the *Raleigh* and the *Ranger*, for the Continental navy.

EPILOGUE

On June 21, 1788, New Hampshire became the ninth state to approve the United States Constitution. Individual towns in New Hampshire have kept a great deal of political power. The modern state legislature includes more than 400 elected representatives, because each town still has the right to elect its own.

New Hampshire has a population of just over one million. About a quarter of the people are of French Canadian origin. Blacks, Asian Americans, and Hispanic Americans combined make up less than one percent of the state population. Half the people live in the state's small cities. Manchester is the largest at 100,000. Next are Nashua, Portsmouth, Rochester, and Concord, the capital.

One New Hampshire worker in four is employed in manufacturing. Two percent of the work force is employed in farming. Farm products include dairy cows, beef cattle, hogs, poultry, hay, apples, and maple syrup. Manufactured goods include electronic and computer equipment, machine parts, lumber, and paper products. Granite is mined in the upland region around Concord. Portsmouth remains New Hampshire's major seaport. Dartmouth College, founded in 1769 in Hanover, has a nationwide reputation.

At one time, settlers had cleared half of New Hampshire's forests. As the economy changed and people gave up farming, trees grew back, so that 85% of the land is again forested. Deer, moose, bear, and beaver still live in New Hampshire's forests. White pine remains the most valuable kind of tree.

More than four million people visit New Hampshire each year to hike, ski, and enjoy the scenery of the White Mountains, and to boat and fish on the many lakes. More than 200 summer camps for children are located in New Hampshire.

New Hampshire's colonial and Revolutionary history are preserved at Strawbery Banke, a restored colonial waterfront neighborhood in Portsmouth; the remains of Fort Constitution—formerly Fort William and Mary—at New Castle; and Fort at Number Four, a reconstructed fortified village of King George's War at Charlestown.

Right: The so-called "Old Man of the Mountain," a rock formation shaped like a profile in the White Mountains of New Hampshire, was a major tourist attraction until it collapsed in 2003.

DATELINE

1524: Giovanni da Verrazano explores the coast of New England.

1605: Sir George Waymouth sails along the New England coast from Nantucket to Maine, and brings five Native Americans back to England.

1614: Captain John Smith explores and maps the New England coast. His book about his voyage promotes interest in the area as a potential colony.

1620: King James I of England sets up the Council of New England to supervise the settlement and government of the territory. The Pilgrims sail on the Mayflower from the Netherlands to Massachusetts and found a colony at Plymouth.

1621: Sir Ferdinando Gorges and Captain John Mason receive a grant of land in northern New England. They form the Laconia Company to finance settlement and exploration of their territory.

1623: The Laconia Company begins sending settlers to the banks of New Hampshire's Piscataqua River.

1629: Mason and Gorges dissolve the Laconia Company and split the territory between them, with Mason keeping the portion which he names New Hampshire, and Gorges keeping the part that becomes Maine.

1630: Puritans from England establish the Massachusetts Bay Colony. Massachusetts settlers soon begin moving north to New Hampshire, and the Massachusetts authorities begin governing New Hampshire.

1680: New Hampshire becomes a royal colony, separate from Massachusetts.

1685: King James II merges Massachusetts Bay, Plymouth, New Hampshire, and Maine into a single colony called the Dominion of New England, with Sir Edmund Andros as the royal governor.

1703–1713: During Queen Anne's War, Native Americans again mount raids against New Hampshire settlements.

DECEMBER 1774: Acting on a warning from Paul Revere, 400 New Hampshire men seize Fort William and Mary, near Portsmouth, to prevent British soldiers from reinforcing it.

AUGUST 1775: New Hampshire's royal governor flees the colony.

1776: New Hampshire forms a new government, and by September declares itself an independent state.

JUNE 21, 1788: New Hampshire becomes the ninth state to approve the United States Constitution.

GLOSSARY

ACT: law, so called because it is made by an act of government

ALLIES: people or nations who have agreed to cooperate, or to fight on the same side in a war

ANGLICAN: Church of England, a Protestant church and the state church of England

BOYCOTT: agreement to refuse to buy from or sell to certain businesses

BRITISH: the nationality of a person born in Great Britain; people born in England are called "English"

CHARTER: a document containing the rules for running an organization

CONGREGATIONAL: church organized by Puritans, based on the idea that each congregation governed itself without interference from a central authority

DUTIES: taxes collected on goods brought into a country

FRONTIER: newest place of settlement, located the farthest away from the center of population

FREEMAN: man who was white and at least 21 years old, and who had the right to vote or hold office

GARRISON: soldiers stationed at a fort to protect it

GREAT BRITAIN: nation formed by England, Wales, Scotland, and Northern Ireland; the term "Great Britain" came into use when England and Scotland formally unified in 1707.

HERESY: belief that is denounced by one's church

INDIAN: name given to all Native Americans at the time Europeans first came to America, because it was believed that America was actually a close neighbor of India

MILITIA: group of citizens not normally part of the army who join together to defend their land in an emergency

MONOPOLY: exclusive right to control the purchase and sale of specific goods or services

NATIVE AMERICAN: member of numerous groups of people who had been living in America for thousands of years at the time that the first Europeans arrived

NEW WORLD: western hemisphere of Earth, including North America, Central America, and South America; so called because the people of the Old World, in Europe, did not know about the existence of the Americas until the 1400s

PARLIAMENT: legislature of Great Britain

PATENT: official document giving someone the right to use a piece of land or permission to conduct a business

PATRIOT: American who wanted the colonies to be independent of Great Britain

PLANTATION: colony or newly planted settlement

PRIVATEER: privately owned ship with government permission to attack the ships of enemy nations during wartime

PROTESTANT: any Christian church that has broken away from Roman Catholic or Eastern Orthodox control

PURITAN: Protestant who wanted the Church of England to practice a more "pure" form of Christianity

SACHEM: Algonquian word for chief

SASSAFRAS: type of tree whose bark is used for flavoring or medical purposes

SMUGGLING: secretly and illegally trading in forbidden merchandise, or hiding goods to avoid paying taxes on them

TITLE: claim to a piece of property

FURTHER READING

Brenner, Barbara. *If You Were There in 1776*. New York: Bradbury Press, 1994.

Carter, Alden R. *Colonies in Revolt*. New York: Franklin Watts, 1988.

Collier, Christopher, and James Lincoln Collier. *The French and Indian War, 1660–1763*. Tarrytown, N.Y.: Marshall Cavendish Corp., 1998.

Smith, Carter, ed. *Battles in a New Land: A Source Book on Colonial America*. Brookfield, Conn.: Millbrook Press, 1991.

Smith, Carter, ed. *Daily Life: A Source Book on Colonial America*. Brookfield, Conn.: Millbrook Press, 1991.

Smith, Carter, ed. *Explorers and Settlers: A Source Book on Colonial America*. Brookfield, Conn.: Millbrook Press, 1991.

Tunis, Edwin. *Colonial Living*. Baltimore: Johns Hopkins University Press, 1999.

Wilbur, C. Keith. *The New England Indians*. Chester, Conn.: Globe Pequot Press, 1990.

WEBSITES

http://www.americaslibrary.gov
Select "Jump back in time" for links to history activities.

http://www.fortat4.org/
Visit the website of Fort at Number Four, a reconstructed fortified New Hampshire village.

http://www.thinkquest.org/library/JR_index.html
Explore links to numerous student-designed sites about American colonial history.

BIBLIOGRAPHY

Daniell, Jere R. *Colonial New Hampshire: A History*. Millwood, N.Y.: KTO Press, 1981.

Hanson, Charles Lane, ed. *A Journal for the Years 1739–1803 by Samuel Lane of Stratham, New Hampshire*. Concord: New Hampshire Historical Society, 1937.

Hawke, David Freeman. *Everyday Life in Early America*. New York: Harper & Row, 1988.

Middleton, Richard. *Colonial America: A History, 1607–1760*. Cambridge, Mass.: Blackwell, 1992.

Morison, Elizabeth Forbes, and Elting E. Morison. *New Hampshire: A Bicentennial History*. New York: W.W. Norton, 1976.

Taylor, Alan. *American Colonies*. New York: Viking, 2001.

The American Heritage History of the Thirteen Colonies. New York: American Heritage, 1967.